With warm friendly thoughts。

Fondly
Cynthia Holt Cummings

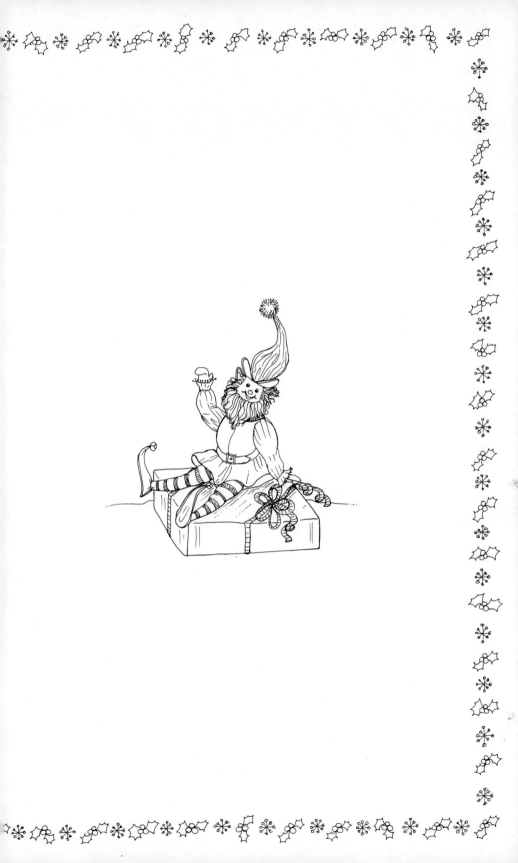

Christmas Memories

poems by Cynthia Holt Cummings
illustrations by Lisa Peterson Rye

Holt Peterson Press
Suite 300
770 S. Adams Rd.
Birmingham, MI 48011

Other books by Holt Peterson Press:

<u>Christmas Ribbons</u>
first printing l979
second printing l980
third printing l981
fourth printing l982

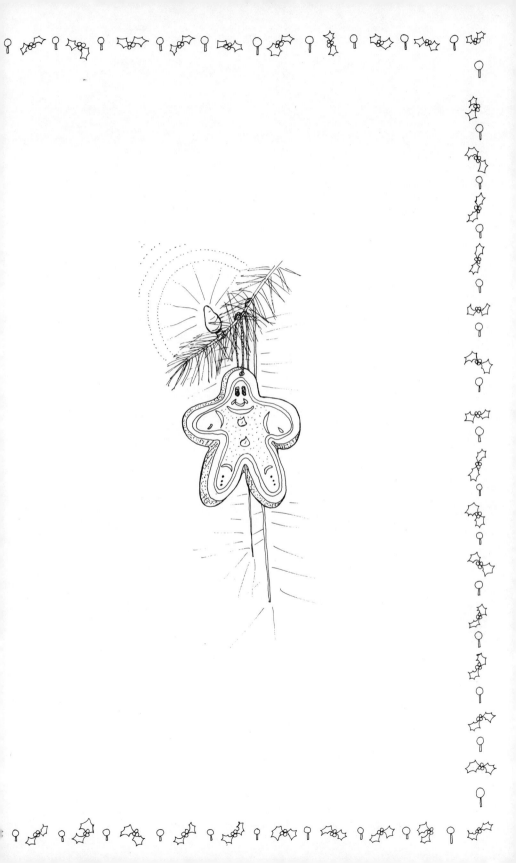

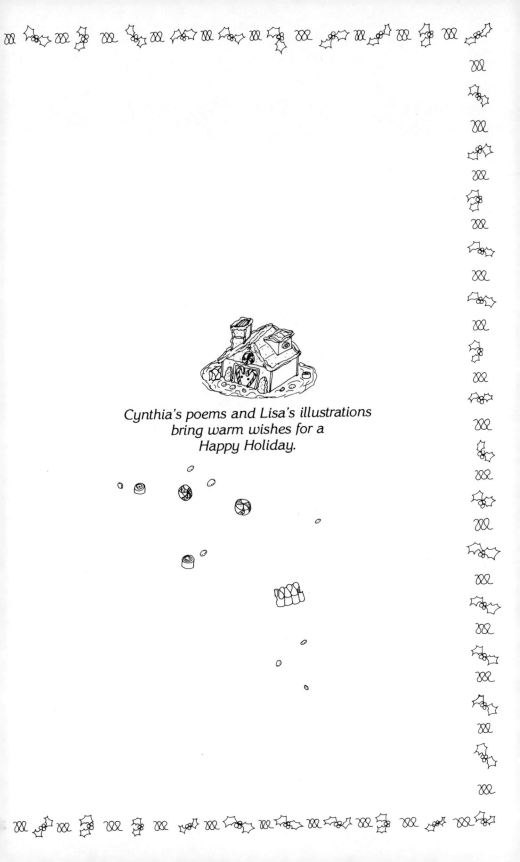

*Cynthia's poems and Lisa's illustrations
bring warm wishes for a
Happy Holiday.*

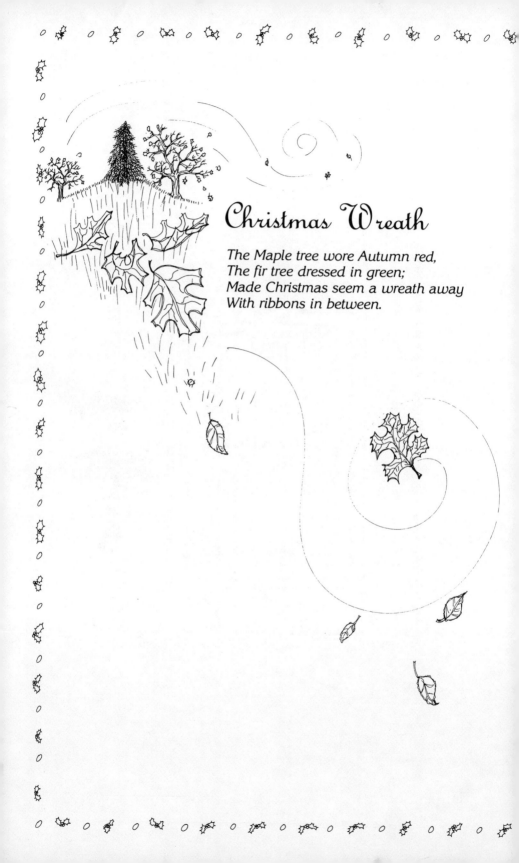

Christmas Wreath

The Maple tree wore Autumn red,
The fir tree dressed in green;
Made Christmas seem a wreath away
With ribbons in between.

Holly

In winter time
The birds are fed
With holly berries of Christmas red.

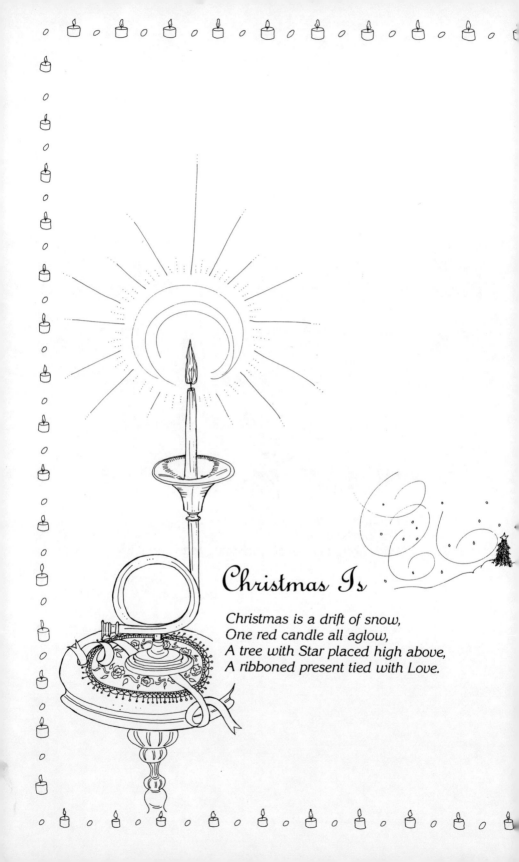

Christmas Is

Christmas is a drift of snow,
One red candle all aglow,
A tree with Star placed high above,
A ribboned present tied with Love.

The Little Church

The little church still stands,
In the small New England town;
And the steeple white,
Is lit with light;
And Christmas is all around.

Winter Morning

There's a stillness in the morning
Until the birds take wing.
Flying so high · Touching the sky,
Making the Heavens sing.

Winter Shawl

A pattern of lace in each Snowflake,
Only God knows the design;
Making a Shawl in December,
To last thru the Wintertime.

The Violet

Blushing pink, a violet
Looked out the windowpane.
And laughed to see the snowflakes
As Winter howled again.

Her color like a blushing bride
Spread over velvet leaves of green.
Displayed to Winter snow outside
What being warm inside could mean.

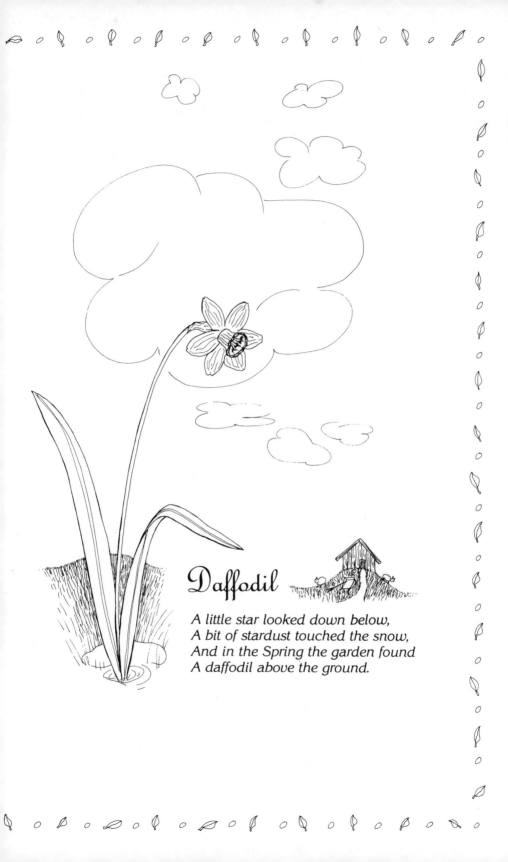

Daffodil

A little star looked down below,
A bit of stardust touched the snow,
And in the Spring the garden found
A daffodil above the ground.

Thank You God

*Thank you God for giving me
Another year to trim the tree.*

The Star
that
Shines so Bright

Walk With Me

Walk with me this Christmas;
See the lights aglow,
Reflecting Christmas Greetings
In the Winter snow.
Peace and Love are all around;
There's music in the air,
Voices singing carols, echo everywhere.
Walk with me this Christmas;
See the glowing star,
Sending out its message
To friends both near and far.
Be thankful in your heart again
For Peace on Earth,
Good Will to men.

The Friendly Hand

This Christmas may there friendly, be —
A neighbor's hand stretched out to me.
If only in a bright porch light
That shows the shape of trees at night;
Or when the window shade is drawn
Upwards to greet the sun that morn;
To let me know that someone's there
Across the road which we both share.
The friendly gesture showing why
The Star that night is in the sky.

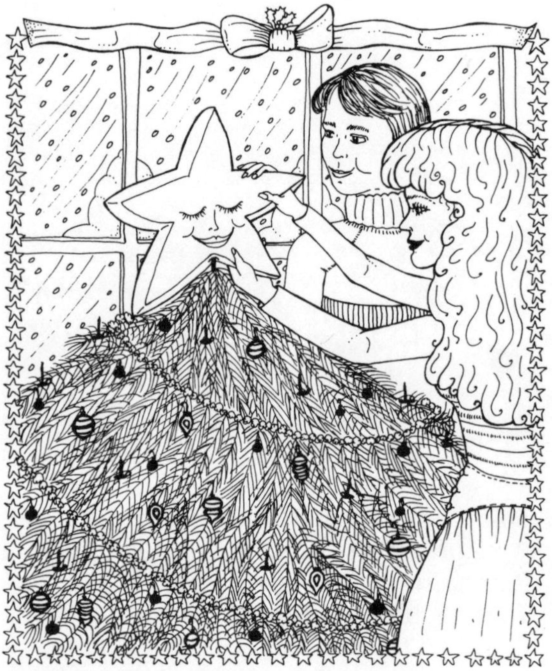

I Bring You Love

I bring you Love, she said to me,
To put beneath the Christmas Tree.
I nurtured it the whole year long
With notes I heard from each bird's song.
And when a child would smile at me
I gathered Love for the family.
Strange how Love can grow and grow
To mingle with a flake of snow.
The wrapping was not hard to find;
I could not pick just any kind.
I searched my heart, and with a kiss,
It took one hug for all of this.
I place it in your tender care,
To put beneath the tree right there.
While up above the Star so bright,
Received her Love on Christmas night.

No Matter What . . .

No matter what may change
Christmas never will.
The star will still glow bright;
There will be pine upon the hill.

No matter what may change
Christmas will remain the same.
We will bow our heads in prayer
And repeat His sacred name.

Christmas Is Over

They say that Christmas is over,
The tree is down;
The colored lights have gone out
All over town.
The red ribboned wreaths
Have left every door
And no rushing crowd
Fills every store;
But if you look high
On a cold winter night,
You can still see the star
Shining so bright.

Peace

May the green of fir
And the gold of light
Bring Peace to All
This Christmas Night.

Dreams
of
Yesterday

It's such a simple thing,
Remembering —

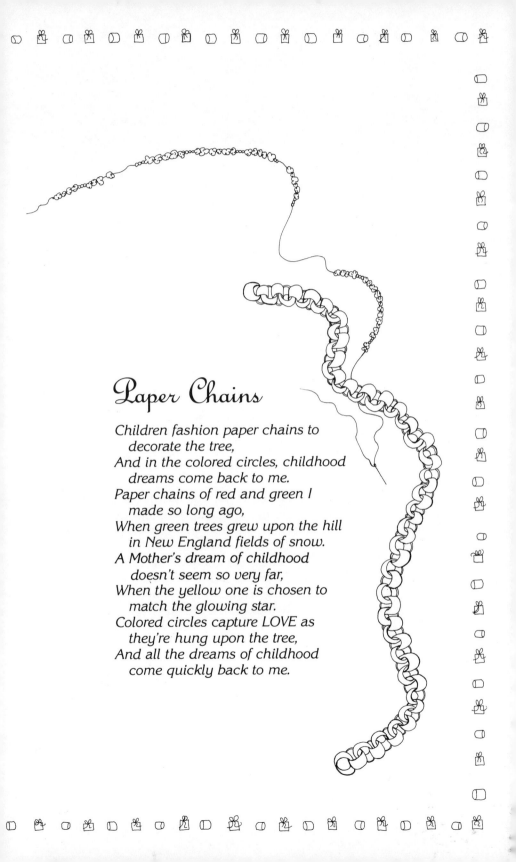

Paper Chains

Children fashion paper chains to
  decorate the tree,
And in the colored circles, childhood
  dreams come back to me.
Paper chains of red and green I
  made so long ago,
When green trees grew upon the hill
  in New England fields of snow.
A Mother's dream of childhood
  doesn't seem so very far,
When the yellow one is chosen to
  match the glowing star.
Colored circles capture LOVE as
  they're hung upon the tree,
And all the dreams of childhood
  come quickly back to me.

Christmas Stocking

Between the age of three and four
I hung a stocking Mother wore . . . .
No fancy trim, just pinned to the chair
To be ready and waiting for Santa there.
On Christmas morn I'd quickly look
To find a brand new coloring book . . . .
A pencil box with tiny key
Would fill the stocking to the knee.
Walnuts and an orange round
Were safely tucked below . . . .
And when I stretched my hand way down
Pennies filled the toe.

Mother's Gifts

In her lap a piece of linen
With an intricate design;
I would often see my mother
Making gifts for Christmastime.

From the strands of colored floss
She could make the flowers bloom;
She was growing summer's garden
Just to warm a winter room.

Threading needles by the hour
With each stitch a bit of love;
She gave roses in December
When the Star was high above.

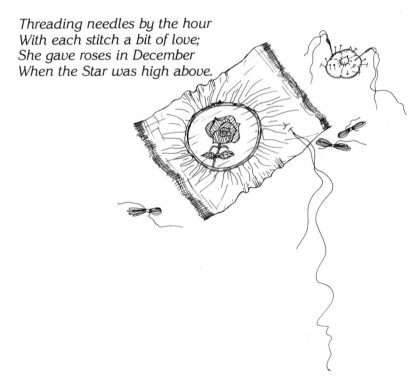

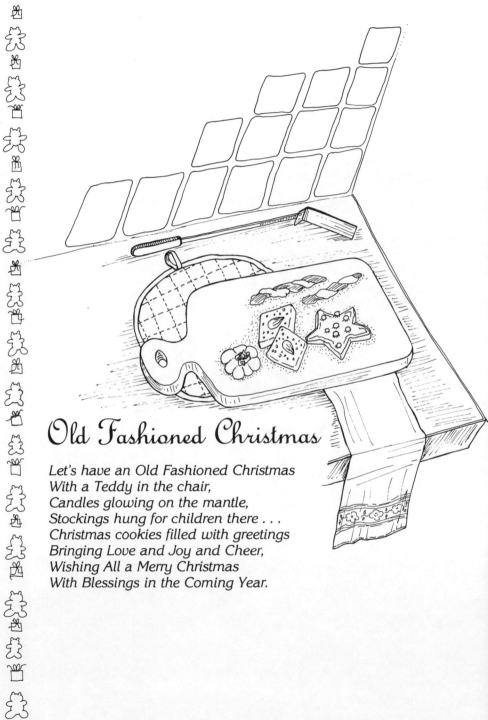

Old Fashioned Christmas

Let's have an Old Fashioned Christmas
With a Teddy in the chair,
Candles glowing on the mantle,
Stockings hung for children there . . .
Christmas cookies filled with greetings
Bringing Love and Joy and Cheer,
Wishing All a Merry Christmas
With Blessings in the Coming Year.

Grandchildren

Where are the children?
Where have they gone?
I once heard their laughter,
I once heard their song.

There are toys in the attic,
Toys in the hall,
Toys in big boxes,
For children so small.

Bring me the dolls.
Wind up the train.
They're coming home
With children again.

Find the toy soldier,
Once shiny and new.
Bring me the tea set
Of China so blue.

I'll polish the table.
I'll place every chair,
With joy in my heart,
With the children there.

Where are the children?
Where have they gone?
Once more I'll hear laughter,
Once more I'll hear song.

Christmas Colors

Grandchildren legs are stretched on
   the floor;
Hands are coloring, books once more.
Green for the tree and gold for the star;
Thoughts of Christmas are not very far.
Santa's suit is a bright, bright red;
His boots are shiny black.
All of this in a coloring book,
Bringing a Christmas back.

How much more love
    could a Christmas card hold,
Than when written by the hand
    of a 3-year old?

The Gold Band

She held the ribbons in her hand
Of red and green and blue,
She looked beneath the tree and saw
The presents that were new.

The little china figurine
The pretty light blue vase,
Reminded her of years gone by
Spent in a different place.

The sun was setting in the West
Upon a field of snow,
And once again she knew so well
That Christmas Day must go.

Among the colored ribbons
She saw the plain gold band,
And realized the love she had
Was held there in her hand.

Memories

The tree is new with branches green;
It stands so straight and tall.
I see the children once again
When they were very small.

I'm hanging Christmas ornaments
To decorate the tree.
In fading colors once so bright
I'm hanging memory.

The little angel still has wings
With a halo made of gold.
The china bell no longer rings
But in it's silence holds,
The memories I now recall
When all the children were so small,
And laughter echoed in the hall.

A Childhood Dream

Memories come and memories go
In candlelight and falling snow;
Blinking lights on every tree
Reflect a childhood dream to me.

The first new sled beneath the tree —
Adventure for a child of three.
Up and down the hill I'd go
To pull the tiny sled in snow.
My laughter echoed in the air —
Childhood dreams were everywhere.
Oh to be a child once more,
To set the spirit free;
To travel back to Winterland
When I was only three.
To see the hills with childhood eyes,
To feel the falling snow;
To build a childhood dream once more
How quickly I would go.

Memories come and memories go
In candlelight and falling snow.
Blinking lights on every tree
Reflect a childhood dream to me.

Love Song

I'm writing a love song for Christmas
As I look at the beautiful tree.
I'm remembering scenes from
   my childhood
With the love of my family.

I'm stringing ropes of red cranberries
To hang 'neath the star of gold.
Oh the wonderful memories of childhood
A love song for Christmas can hold.

I can hear the chime of the church bells
Echoing over the hill.
I can see Santa's sleigh on its journey
With so many stockings to fill.

And as candles glowed in each window
And the snowflakes came falling down —
We would sing Christmas carols to
   the shut-ins
In that little country town.

The laughter and love in my childhood
That all of this could be mine —
To share in a love song for Christmas
With others this Christmastime.

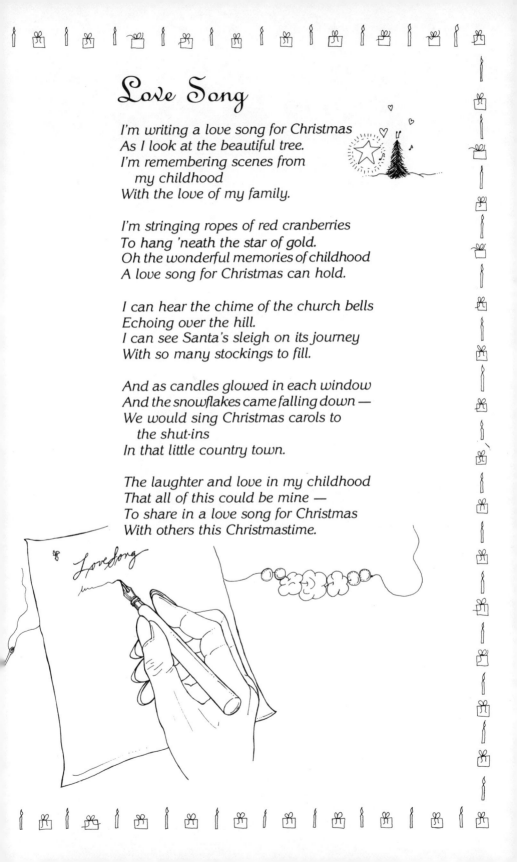

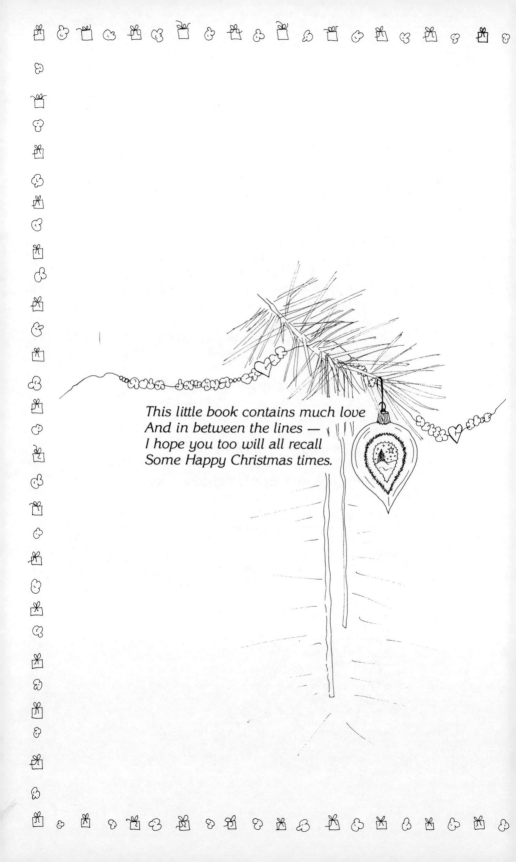

This little book contains much love
And in between the lines —
I hope you too will all recall
Some Happy Christmas times.

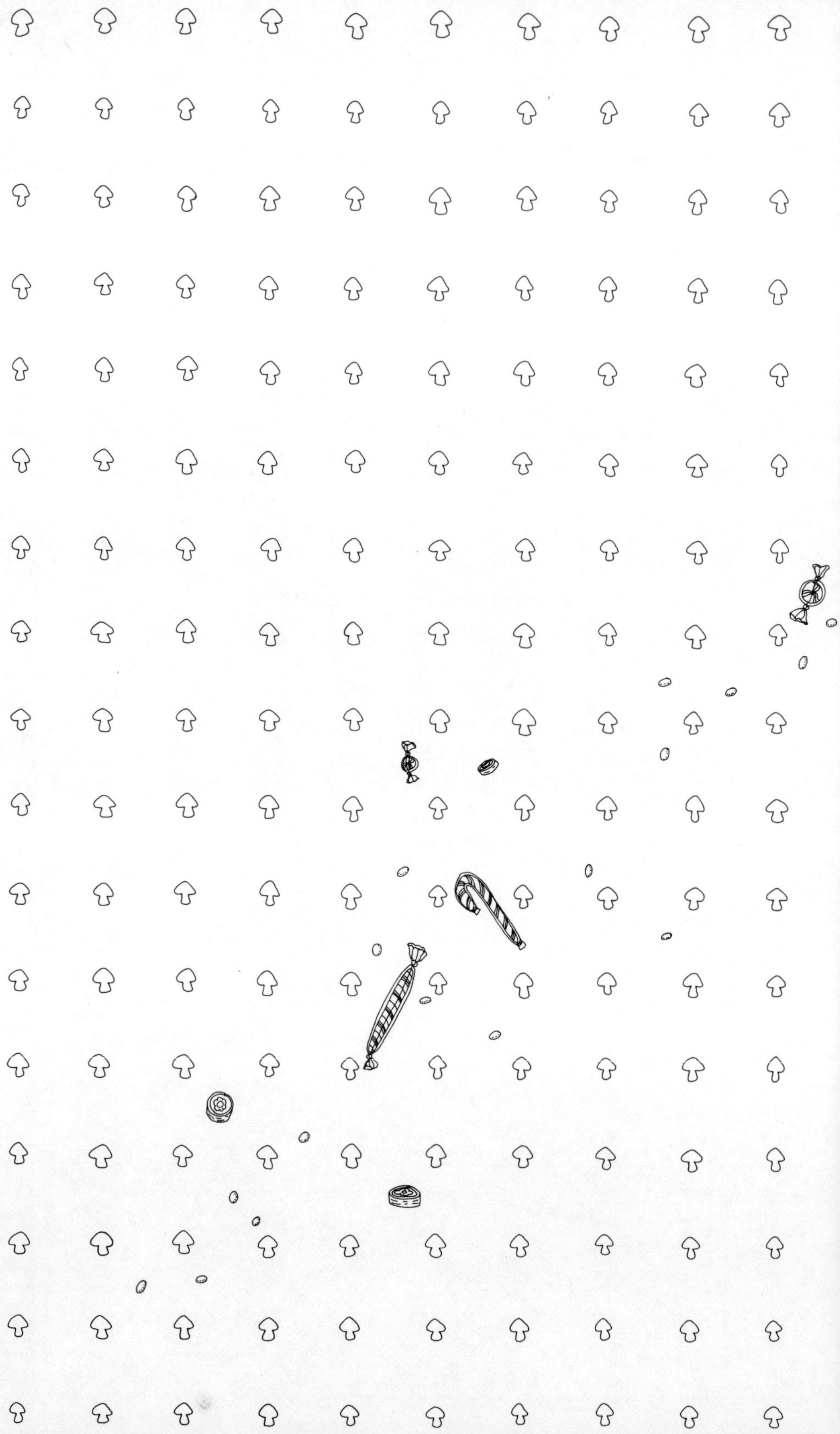

Visions
of
Sugarplums

When you teach a child to pray
You give him love for each new day.

The Walking Doll

The walking doll was looking up,
Looking up to see ·
The beautiful star · the beautiful star
At the top of the Christmas tree.

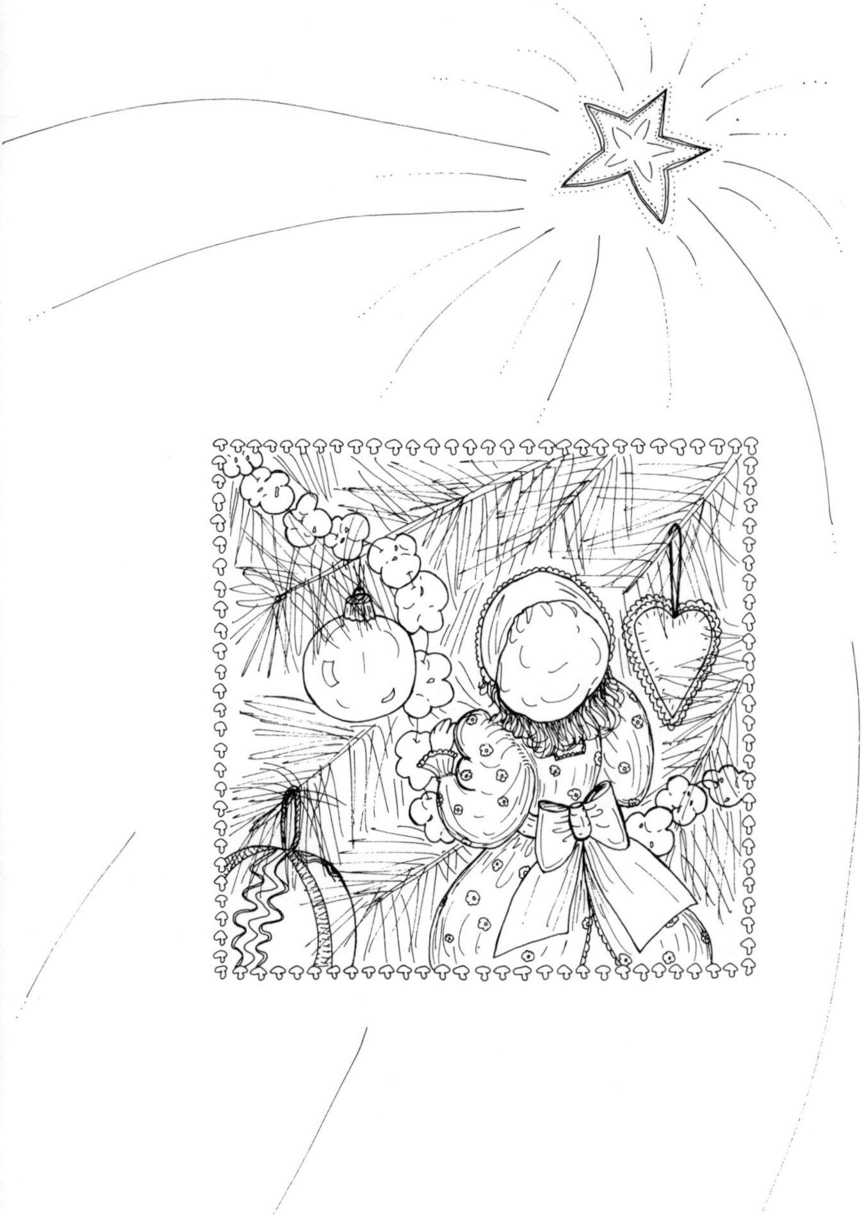

The little toy soldier opened his eyes
Then stood up straight and tall.
He turned his head and then he saw
The lovely walking doll.
Now the walking doll had never seen
A soldier in red and blue.
She quickly turned her head away
Not knowing what to do.

Just take my hand the soldier said,
No reason to be afraid.
The Star will guide us with its light,
That's why stars were made.

The music box began to play
As the doll took the soldier's hand;
And that is the way the star will say
The Christmas Ball began.
The ornaments were swaying
And the bells began to chime.
The presents danced beneath the tree ·
They were having a merry time.

Dancing and dancing around the tree,
The soldier in red and blue,
Held in his arms a walking doll
Who knew her love would be true.
The beautiful star at the top of the tree
Looked down on the pair below;
Giving its blessing to each of them
With its Christmas starlit glow.

As Christmases would come and go
The soldier in blue and red,
Would look at the lovely walking doll
With the star high overhead.
And the walking doll would remember
A Christmas long ago,
Standing beside a Christmas tree
Under the starlit glow;
When a soldier had said ·
Just take my hand,
No reason to be afraid.
The star will guide us with its light,
That's why stars were made.

Santa's Dream

Santa's dream for Christmas ·
For every face a smile,
Pockets filled with laughter
To give to every child.

Merry, Merry Christmas
Echoes from the snow,
Peace lights every window
With candles all aglow.

Santa's dream for Christmas ·
The star so high above
Will welcome in the New Year,
Fill every home with LOVE.

The Little Bear

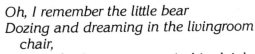

Oh, I remember the little bear
Dozing and dreaming in the livingroom
chair,
Waiting for Santa to come in his sleigh
To bring him some honey for Christmas
Day.
Resting his chin on his tiny paws
His head held visions of Santa Claus.
All year long he had been very good
In just the way that little bears should.
Now, Santa had heard of the little bear
Dozing and dreaming in the livingroom
chair.
So, in his sleigh he put that nite
A jar of honey with ribbons bright.
On the tag he wrote with care ·
From Santa Claus to my favorite bear.

The Toys' Celebration

Rocking and Rocking, the little horse
Was waiting for Christmas morn;
Rocking, Rocking, he waited and
*   listened*
For the sound of the Soldier's horn.
The Jack-in-the-Box raised his head,
We must hurry before they wake;
And the little horse just rocked and
*   rocked*
Then gave his tail a shake.

The little toy soldier blew his horn
And the notes came loud and clear;
The dolls were ready to take their bows
As the Teddy Bear gave a cheer.
The little train just puffed and puffed
Around the track on the floor,
And the lion began to roll about
Then gave a mighty roar.

On the top of the tree the little Star
Was as happy as could be,
Never before had there been such a sight
Beneath the Christmas Tree.
The music box began to play
And the dolls all clapped their hands,
And the Rocking Horse just rocked and
    rocked
To the rhythm of the band.

The Toylike celebration
Was a special sight to see,
And the little Star just glowed and
*   glowed*
At the top of the Christmas Tree.

The Rocking Horse became *very* still
And he turned his head to hear;
I hear a noise, Be quiet, Be quiet,
The children will soon be near.
The music box was all run down
And the Lion was fast asleep,
And everyone was back in place
With the secrets they would keep.
Oh look · Oh look, the children cried,
What a beautiful sight to see;
And the only one that was still awake
Was the Star on the Christmas tree.

The Candy Cane Ballet

On a stage of snow under starlit glow,
The Candy Canes began to dance;
And the music of the whistling wind
Could be heard thru every branch.
Of all the trees in the forest there
Standing so straight and tall,
Watching the Candy Cane Ballet
As Christmas came to call.

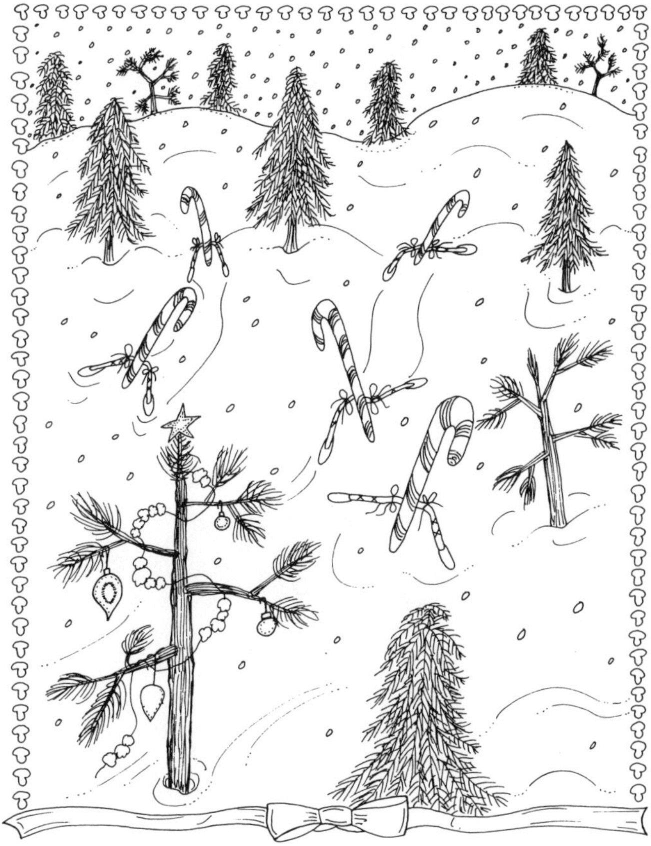

The Squirrels and the Rabbits
Were as quiet as could be,
For a Candy Cane Ballet
Was a special sight to see.
Louder and louder the whistling wind
Whistled thru the trees,
Faster and faster the dancers spun
Bowing to their knees.

Suddenly the candy canes became so
    very still,
As the morning sun was rising
Over the snow-capped hill.
The whistling wind became quiet,
And the Rabbits scampered away,
And the Squirrels followed quickly
For this was Christmas Day.

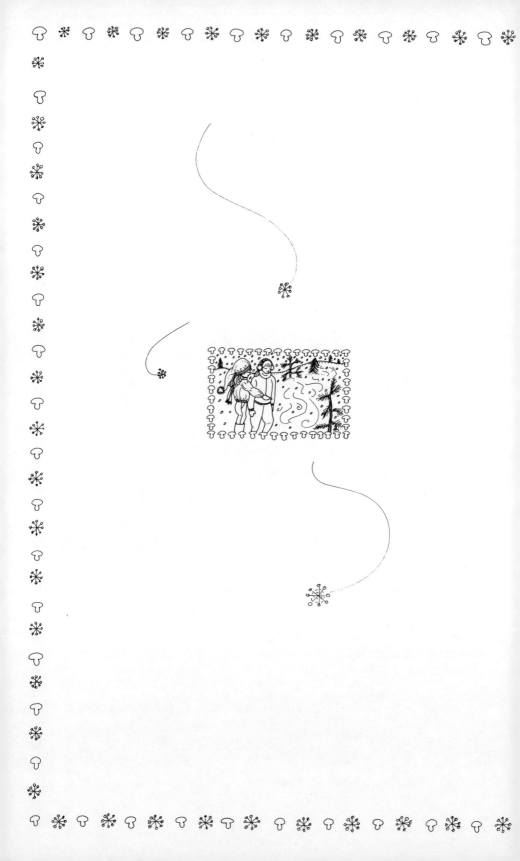

The children say
In the town that day
The people all were talking,
About lacey patterns in the snow
They had seen when they were walking.

Don't Forget

Time to take the tree down and put
  the things away;
But don't forget to keep quite near
The LOVE you'll give thru out the year.

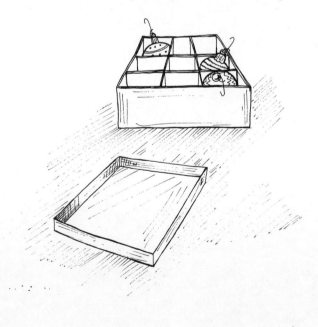

About the Author

Cynthia Holt Cummings, a resident of West Bloomfield, Michigan, was born in West Boylston, Massachusetts. Upon graduation from Massachusetts General Hospital Training School for Nurses, she joined the hospital's 6th General Hospital reserve unit as a second lieutenant in the Army Nurse Corps. Shortly after World War II began, the hospital unit departed for active duty, spending thirty-three months in North Africa and Italy.

She later married Richard Howe Cummings. Their son Roger Holt Cummings, named after her youngest brother an Air Force gunner killed during the war, is married to Buff with two children . . . David and Julie.

About the Illustrator

Lisa Peterson Rye is a freelance designer and illustrator, working out of her studio in Birmingham, Michigan. Married to Jonathan, and living in Bloomfield Township, she is currently illustrating greeting cards for various card companies and organizations.

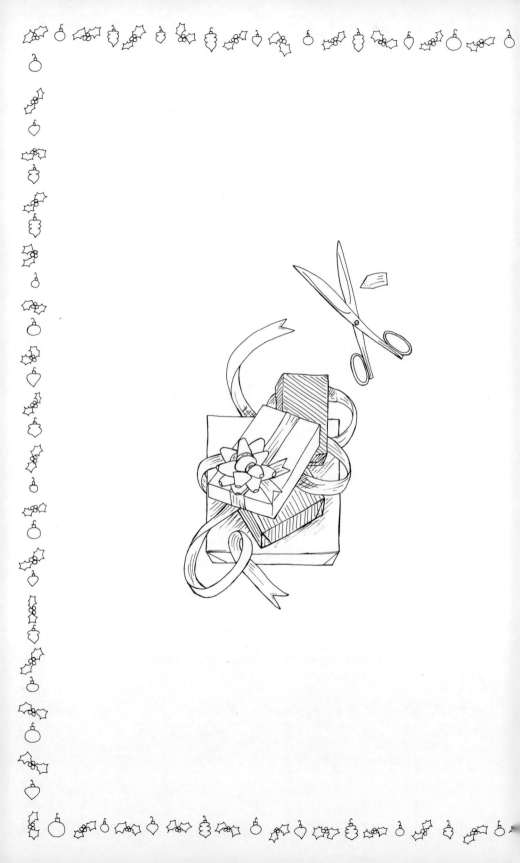